THE LEAN EXPLAINER VIDEO

A Video Production Handbook for Startups and
Entrepreneurs

By Dan Englander

SalesSchema.com

Table of Contents

1. Getting Started

The IdeaRocket team and I were well into production on the show opener for the eighth and final season of *Weeds,* Showtime's sitcom about a suburban housewife turned marijuana kingpin. Over the weekend, Will Gadea, our creative director, and Robert Kopecky, our principal designer, binged on every episode. Now the guys were distilling their newfound knowledge into a concept that told the story of protagonist Nancy Botwin, traversing her journey from her San Fernando Valley beginnings, to her bloody run-ins with Mexican cartels, to her eventual move to Old Sandwich, Connecticut. For this tale, our creatives employed an all-digital whiteboard animation approach, which allowed for splashes of color, a green-screened drawing hand, and subtle character movements, all playing out to the tune of Malvina Reynolds' "Little Houses". After constructive feedback from the show's creator and producers, the opener was a hit. We got coverage on the major industry blogs, and we were nominated for the Excellence in Title Design award at South By Southwest.

I was stoked, but it felt like the project pulled us away from our roots as a full-service explainer video studio. Before the *Weeds* job, our clients were almost entirely tech startups and complex business offerings. Then it occurred to me: We had created an explainer video for the series. Like all of our business video productions, the *Weeds* opener rested on characters and a story.

I was proud of the work because it did something different than most openers: It educated the audience. Though an uninitiated viewer might need to fill in some blanks after seeing the opener, she would leave with conceptual understanding for everything that had happened up until the eighth season. The intro took new viewers by the hand into the chaos of the show. It engaged them while building comfort and familiarity. With that in mind, the complexity Will and Robert communicated was miles above our most intricate tech explainers. Our creatives pulled off this feat without voice over or another stream of audio information. They used no more than a few colors.

The takeaway is that you don't need to overthink your explainer. It doesn't have to rail off every feature and benefit, or bring in all possible audiences. It just has to tell a compelling story, which requires characters in some shape or form. Furthermore, your explainer doesn't have to allay every objection; it just needs to build a base level of trust. Ultimately, your piece has to get your audience hungry for the next part of their journey.

Congrats if you reached the explainer milestone! It's probably an exciting time for you and your company, and chances are you have a million other things on your plate. While explainer production is a good hurdle, it's a hurdle nonetheless. If you're anything like my clients, you're wondering about questions like these:

- How do you create something memorable?
- How do you make sure your video converts?
- How do you find the right balance between quality and cost?
- How do you choose the right producer?
- How do you select the right technique?
- How do you have a smooth production process?

This book will give you relief from all of these worries and many more. While I'm big on the conceptual, we'll also get both nitty and gritty.

The explainer video does not live in the cerebral realm of white papers and sales collateral. Rather, it's a neighbor to the music videos, show openers, movies, and super bowl commercials that tug on your heartstrings. When you combine the tried and true magic of good storytelling with your product's powerful message, you'll create your most effective marketing asset.

Let's get into it!

Resources

This is an analog and quasi-digital text on a 100% digital topic: How the hell are we going to make this work? Why, with a resources page, of course!

Throughout the book, I reference "Resources", including tools, spreadsheets, downloadable documents, and other goodies.
To access them, please go here when you're at your computer or mobile device: www.SalesSchema.com/Explainer-Landing

To get these materials, I'm going to ask for your email because I want to ensure you exclusive access. More importantly, you'll receive our newsletter, which is the best way for me to keep you informed about this evolving space. Continual learning is important so you can leverage new strategies, tools, and hacks. You can opt out anytime, and I promise I won't flood your inbox.

Setting Expectations

I wrote this book to give you the strongest framework for creating an awesome high-converting explainer. That being said, the ingredients that go into a compelling script and a seamless production process can just as easily be applied to other video formats and marketing undertakings. If you read my video marketing book, you might be aiming for a different video approach, like a testimonial, PSA, or walkthrough.

This book is *not* a do-it-yourself instruction manual, nor is it a technical course on video editing. Although we'll touch on a few DIY video platforms, that's not our main focus. If you're a startup or entrepreneur, your time is valuable   Producing an awesome *homemade* explainer is probably not realistic. Settling for a low-quality stick figure promo will most likely do more harm than good. So instead of spinning your wheels and hurting your brand, you'll learn how to (A) build the foundation for your video (your message, script, and voice over), and (B) hire out production to the pros in a highly cost-effective way. If you're tight for funds, you might choose to save a bit of money handling your script, voice over, or storyboard yourself. You'll learn how to do that later.

Why Video?

As Comscore found, the average viewer watches 32.2 videos per month, and that web video as a whole is experienced by 100 million viewers per day. Granted, a fair slice of that is probably cat videos, so why does this matter for your business explainer? According to Forbes, 50% of CEOs watch business-related videos on a frequent basis, and 65% visit the company's site after viewing. The simple act of adding an explainer to an email can increase click-through rates by 200-300%, according to Forrester Marketing Group.

We can go anecdotal. Before Dropbox was the cloud storage leader we know today, they were a fledgling company in a competitive space. The simple act of adding an explainer to their homepage brought them 10% more leads, and a revenue increase of $48 million (source: Switch Video). At IdeaRocket, we experienced a 46% lead increase when we added our homepage video.

If you read marketing blogs, you might be sick of stats like these. I'm probably not the first person to beat you over the head with data-driven reasons to invest in this medium.

At the end of the day, we don't need dry case studies. From movies and TV, the strength of this medium is intuitive, and you're probably sold on it already. Forgive me for reselling you; I want you to be confident that your energy is heading in the right direction.

Quality Vs. Cost

Pop in your Third Eye Blind CD, zip up your baggy pants, and step into my time machine! We're zooming back to the late 90s and early 2000s, when the Internet was in its infancy. Marketing gurus raved that it was imperative for all business entities to create websites. Within a year or two, thousands of pages sprung up. Many site creators thought the Internet could represent a radical departure from the best marketing practices of the last 100 years. They neglected quality design, buyer psychology, and customer experience. The result was a dull landscape of low-quality, homogenous sites.

Over time, businesses began to realize that the above considerations are important online in the same way they had been offline, as applied to mediums like billboards, brochures, and television commercials. Eventually we achieved today's vibrant and visually diverse digital landscape.

Let's go back to the future. When it comes to the state of web video, doesn't it feel like the early days of the internet? An echo chamber of marketers, including yours truly, rails off about the importance of video. "Create one immediately or you'll be left in the dust," we say. In the face of this pressure, it's tempting to repeat the mistakes of the past and rush into creating something prefabricated or formulaic, based on the models of *this* or *that* successful company.

Deceptive case studies about the success of certain stick figure explainers make it seem like quality should be an afterthought. As a result, intelligent marketers are often misled into producing low-quality videos for sophisticated products. This medium is viewed and shared more often than any other content. Quality matters, and its brand implications run deep.

One of the most common questions I hear is, "What's more important, quality or cost?" This is a loaded question. These factors are not mutually exclusive. You should look for the best possible end product for your budget without being fooled into thinking that quality doesn't matter. You might adopt a cost-effective technique that your competitors aren't using. As a last resort, maybe you table your video aspirations until you're in a stronger financial position. Since video will become your message to the world, no explainer is better than a bad one.

Although there are guidelines for a compelling narrative, there's no blueprint for a high-converting explainer. You should take lessons from Dropbox and other successful companies, but don't be afraid to go out on a limb and get creative, or let your producer do that for you. In the next chapters, you'll get the inspiration needed to create a video that stays with your audience.

Animation

Animation is the focus of this book. If you have a complex product, it's probably your ideal approach. Here are reasons why::

- **More Accessible**
  You can start writing your script and storyboarding with no one but yourself, and then you can take your work to a professional for design, animation and sound. Or you can hire out the whole process and come to the table with nothing but your knowledge and experience. Regardless, the barrier to entry is low in comparison to live action.

- **Shorter Production Time**
  Though animation is time-intensive, it's a smaller commitment than shooting live action. A big part of that is not having to deal with a cast and crew.

- **Less Expensive**
  Price ranges can vary depending on quality, which we'll get into shortly, but overall, technology has made animation more affordable than it once was. Unless you're using a cheap iPhone setup, live action is usually a big spend.

- **Better for Handling Complexity**
  Because the approach offers two independent streams of audio and visual information, it's excellent for encapsulating complex thoughts and ideas, from the nuts and bolts of your product to the subtle nuances of

your brand. You can leverage icons, schematics, and other visual effects to get your message across.

- **More Real Than Real**
  It's often easier for us to envision ourselves in fictional roles than it is as the real human in front of us. Actors, if they're not super talented, can feel rather untrustworthy or distant. Animated characters, on the other hand, feel right at home.

- **Fun and Non-Intimidating**
  Although there are many professional-looking animation styles, the format is playful and it builds comfort. This is important because more often than not, your audience will be facing a problem when they come to you.

- **Fewer Creative Limitations**
  If you can dream it, you can draw it. There are few other mediums where that holds true.

Live Action

There are certain objectives that work better for live action— for example, showing off a physical product, or building trust and familiarity. If your business is especially people-centered, then showing human faces will build the connection you need with your audience.

For this reason, testimonials and culture videos tend to work well in live action. Maybe you want to show off your cool office space so you can attract new talent, or you want to tell an interesting customer story.

This is a generalization, but the approach tends to work better for non-complex products because of its visual limitations; you don't have the luxury of icons and screenshots as you do in animation.

Live action tends to involve more time and energy. You or your producer must handle casting, scheduling, lighting, camera crews, editing, waivers, and a ton of other things. It's tougher to get started on your own with this approach unless you have the right know-how and equipment.

Takeaways

There's no marketing medium more powerful than video. The data, and probably your experience, back that up. Chances are you've enjoyed movies, television, commercials, and web videos your whole life. In comparison to any other marketing medium, you're born an expert. So don't overthink this space. Although there are features, benefits, user journeys, and other factors to contend with, your explainer is simply an opportunity to tell your story. For now, take a second to consider, on a gut level, whether animation or live action will best carry your message.

From there, you might be wondering what you should spend on your video. Who should you hire? What goes into comparing providers? The producer marketplace is crowded, and in the next chapter, you'll learn how to navigate it.

2. Producers

I have good news and bad news: The good news is that you have literally hundreds of options for selecting a producer. The bad news is the same as the good.

Web video's boom draws new providers into the marketplace every day. A professional video is no small investment, and this chapter will help you pick the right provider without overspending.

Few companies take the time to evaluate the important elements of the producer work they're evaluating, and as a result they end up with subpar videos. You will avoid this pitfall by zooming in on the aspects that matter. This means taking a close look at scripts, design, animation, sound, and relevant experience. Yes, you'll compare price too, but this will come at the end because it's important to get the lay of the quality landscape first.

From there, you'll learn about pricing structures, overages, and the little cost details that are easy to miss. You'll get leeway for potential discounts. Above all, the task of producer selection will become approachable.

Check out <u>Resources</u> for links and details on video marketplaces and other selection tools.

A La Carte Studios

Video producers generally fall into one of a few different groups. The first, for lack of a better term, are *a la carte*. They produce your video after you provide them a script, and sometimes a storyboard and voice over. These elements combined are known as the *initial creative*. Some full-service studios provide a lower pricing model when you come to the table with these assets.

A la carte providers are generally less expensive than full-service, and the sacrifice is that the creative foundation for your video is in your hands. Rough pricing for a video at 2 minutes or less, in my experience, is up to $10,000. Above that, and you're in the full-service realm.

In later sections, you'll learn the complete process for creating your script so you can approach studios like these with a strong creative foundation.

Full-Service Studios

As you can guess, full-service providers do everything. You come in with your experience, and they write the script, cast and record voice over, and handle design, animation, and sound.

If you go the full-service route, the later chapters will really help you stay ahead of the process and make sure you and your stakeholders can enable your producer to create the best possible explainer.

The full-service floor is somewhere around $3,000 and the high-end is above $20,000. At this ceiling, the quality level should resemble broadcast video.

Freelancers

If you have a limited budget, hiring an independent freelancer might be your best option. Services like Upwork and Fiverr offer a huge array of talent. Freelancer costs can range from less than $100 to several thousand dollars. If you find the right talent, the value can be huge.

On the other hand, there are some challenges. The first is quality level. Make sure your freelancer has an expansive portfolio, and review it carefully based on the areas we'll cover shortly. Prioritize those who can show you an independent portfolio outside of the hiring platform you're using.

Another challenge is language barrier. Many low-cost producers outside the US know limited English. When it comes to run-of-the-mill marketing tasks, this isn't always a big problem, but when you have to communicate subtle creative direction, language barriers cause major headaches. I once had a stressful yet comical experience trying to explain to a group of Indian animators how and why an African American animated character needed to be less racialized. The back and forth was exhausting. After that one-time outsourcing experiment in our early days, we never went out-of-house again.

DIY Animation Platforms

A ton of DIY animation platforms have sprung up recently. They provide intuitive interfaces for creating your own videos. You can use their templates and move around different characters, backgrounds, and text, and upload voice over and music. The quality is low in comparison to a professional option. Most homemade creations are very static, and they often resemble glorified PowerPoints.

I'm not saying that you should absolutely avoid this route. But you should keep both your brand and availability in mind before settling on a homemade solution.

Remember that your video will be the first thing visitors view, click on, and share. With that in mind, ask yourself if a mostly-static stick figure will get the job done. Does your site need to project professionalism? If so, can you risk putting a cheap-looking video smack dab in the middle of it? Your decision will depend on your brand obligations; a sophisticated B2B software product must project a different image than a mobile game for teenagers.

Also, consider how much time will you will invest learning and creating in your DIY platform. If you translated that time into dollars, is it then worth it to hire a pro, and end up with a better video?

If you're leaning toward DIY, PowToon is the current leader. Others include GoAnimate and Devolver. Make sure to write an awesome script, record a high-quality voice over, and rough out a storyboard before you get started. Once these elements are locked down, your process will move along much more smoothly.

While DIY is a questionable move for your main explainer, it's an ideal option for longer product tutorials and walkthroughs, typically those you would record as screencast videos. These assets serve a different purpose than explainers, as they help educate and engage your leads as opposed to onboarding new visitors. If you want to create tutorials, then you probably won't need to hire anything out; you can use software like Camtasia for PC or ScreenFlow for Mac. Both run at around $100, and the learning curve is pretty small.

DIY Live Action

When it comes to explainers and other promotional videos, you should only do live action yourself if you have the equipment and expertise. As we talked about, there are many moving parts involved in professional-looking live action, and the stakes are too high to put out a cheesy iPhone video.

If you're making frequent content videos or educational content, then the quality expectation is lower, and homemade live action might work for you.

Script Evaluation

In the next few sections, you'll learn how to evaluate key video elements so you can make an informed producer decision. To compare work, take some time to watch a few relevant videos from your 3-4 shortlisted producers. As we covered, don't let price cloud your judgement before you've gotten a complete view of the quality landscape. This is kind of like how realtors show potential home buyers properties that are way above and below their budgets before touring ideally-priced homes.

The script is the most important video element. As actors and directors will affirm, if the script sucks, no amount of Academy-quality acting or awe-inspiring special effects will rectify it. This holds true for explainers.

Evaluating scripts will involve listening as much as watching. When comparing producer portfolios, keep these considerations in mind.

- How well do you understand the product by the end of the video?
- How original is the narrative? If it plays out like every other formulaic explainer, with an opening voice over reading, "This is Bob. Bob has a problem. . . .", then it might indicate a lack of imagination.
- Can you remember complex details an hour or more after watching?
- Does the video tell a story?
- Does the story resonate on an emotional level?
- If there are metaphors, do they enhance or detract?

Design Quality

Design can encompass many techniques, which might make it tough to do an apples to apples comparison. Later, you'll learn about styles. For now, let's go into the high-level considerations.

- How memorable is the approach?
- Can you project the visuals in your head after an hour or more?
- How original is it?
- How much detail? Compare it to an example from a DIY platform like PowToon. If you could do it yourself, you probably shouldn't pay a producer more than the value of the time you would spend.
- Are the visuals on-brand? A childish-looking style probably won't work for a complex enterprise software app.

Animation Quality

Animation is the movement of the characters and scenes. As with design, different techniques play out in different ways. That being said, these overarching considerations will help you gauge animation quality.

- How smooth are the scene transitions?
- Does the video progress seamlessly, or are the changes choppy and awkward?
- How much movement is there overall? Is the video lively, or does it feel overly static, like a souped-up PowerPoint?
- How well do the movements add to the drama and storytelling?

- How is the pace? Is it too fast or too slow? The video should leave enough breathing room for the viewer to consume all the information without feeling slow and boring.

Sound Quality

Sound is a huge factor. When you're comparing studios, as well as evaluating video drafts later, make sure to open your ears as much as you open your eyes.

- Does the voice over fit the audience? The gruff old guy who will resonate with a bunch of male auto shop owners probably won't work for an audience of stay-at-home moms.
- How well does the tone carry the message? You probably don't want an academic tone for a fun consumer mobile app.
- Are there sound effects? Do they add to the drama and excitement? This is an element that separates the good videos from the great ones. Many studios completely neglect sound effects, or use one or two cheesy noises, so keep an ear out.
- If there's music, does it fit? Is it used tastefully? Does it enhance or detract? Are you listening to stock or an original score?
- How is the overall sound quality? Is the voice over fighting for dominance over the music? Are the levels consistent? Is the sound crisp and clear, or are there crackles, pops, and other artifacts?

Experience

A base level of experience is important, but don't go overboard looking for a producer that's made a ton of videos in your niche. If your studio has a base level of quality work, chances are they will do just fine for your product. You can envision relevant experience as extra credit. Here's what to keep in mind:

- What is their overall experience?
- How long have they been in business?
- Roughly how many videos do they have under their belt?
- Do they have experience in your industry? If so, what was the context of the project?
- Can they show results? Maybe this is a case study that has metrics on conversions, sales, and traffic.

Pricing

When it comes time to compare pricing, stack up studios based on the above quality areas first. This is important because prices are all over the map, ranging from less than $100 to upwards of $20,000 for a 90-second video. I've seen 5-figure videos from studios with a quality level comparable to amateur freelancers. Take some time to understand quality first, and you'll avoid overpaying. From there, exclude those outside your ballpark to develop a shortlist, just as you would for any other major purchase.

If you don't have a budget yet, consider what you've spent on similar projects, like a minor site redesign or an advertising campaign. Talk to peers in related companies and ask about the gains they've achieved. Thinking conservatively: If you brought in a comparable number of leads, users, or whatever your goal, what would that mean for your bottom line? Estimating your target ROI from the beginning will tell you how much quality you can afford, and it will help you plan for success.

The Fine Print

As with most creative projects, there are cost details and contingencies of which you should be aware before entering the marketplace. Most buyers don't know about these points. This knowledge will put you miles ahead, bringing you major potential savings.

- **Promotional Discounts**
  Some studios will extend a discount if you include a small version of their logo at the end of the video. Sometimes this is only offered if your audience complements your studio. For example, since most producers cater to businesses, they might not extend the discount if you're a consumer app. In addition, you might be asked to link to the studio on your site for SEO purposes.

  Some producers include their logo mandatorily, and then penalize their clients if they want to remove it (I've never understood this tactic). Make sure to talk about promotional considerations with your producer because it might mean a major discount.

- **Length Overages**
  If you contract a 90-second video and it goes to two minutes, most studios will charge overages because the length determines their labor. Typically the

22

charges are on a per-second basis. To avoid overages, make sure to time out your script at each draft stage.

- **Creative Retakes**
Since most studios operate on a flat-rate model, they include protections for excessive edits because without them the occasional problem client could drive them into ruin by demanding excessive redos. Collaboration and revisions are part of the creative process, but given the time-intensive nature of animation, limits are a necessity.

Creative retakes are typically structured in one of two ways. The first is a cap on the number of rounds of revisions. For example, a studio might say that you have up to two rounds on the storyboard, and two on the final animation. After that, they would charge either hourly or flat fees.

The second retake model sets an hourly cap on the total number of retake hours. For example, a studio might allot you 20 hours of creative retakes for every minute of video, and after that they charge an hourly fee. Assuming the cap is high enough, I think this model is best because it ensures that overages are only charged during extreme situations. This keeps penalties from hindering the creative flow between studio and client.

- **Payment Terms**
A typical model is 50 percent upfront and 50 percent after final approval. Keep in mind that some studios

won't deliver completed files until the final payment is received. If you have a slow accounts payable department, or cash flow issues, keep an eye out for this.

- **Time Frame**
  Your producer should give you one, and it will vary depending on the video length and style. That said, 4-8 weeks is typical. The scripting period is the most important part of the process, and it's one you should not rush. Also, scripting requires more feedback and attention from your side. For this reason, some studios base their promised turnaround after the script approval date. IdeaRocket, for example, promises a turnaround of five weeks after script approval.

- **Portfolio Rights**
  Many studios grant themselves a limited right to include your video as part of their portfolio. This usually isn't an issue, and it means a little extra promotion for your completed piece. If, however, your message is non-public, be sure to inform your producer.

Video Producer Marketplaces

Video producer marketplaces offer a helpful turnkey solution for finding and hiring. Most monetize by taking a commision from the studio when they're engaged, and for this reason many producers don't join these hubs. Also, some marketplaces limit your ability to converse with prospective producers before hiring. With all this in mind, you should use a marketplace in conjunction with your independent research.

Here are a few of the top marketplaces:

- **Video Brewery**
  This is the leading site. To start a project, you enter some basic information, input your contact details, submit a $10 deposit, and Video Brewery sources companies.

- **Wooshii**
  This one has a very sleek and intuitive interface. You can use a slider to adjust the length and your budget, and Wooshii gives you a real time estimate for how many proposals you can expect to bid.

- **Vidaao**
  This is more of a listing service, or aggregator. Vidaao is a helpful research tool. You input your location and the site returns a multitude of studios with prices and ratings.

Takeaways

You are distilling your complex product down to a 90-second elevator pitch. Finding the right producer to accomplish this feat is a big decision. Aside from budget constraints, your provider must have the right professionalism and creative chops.

Start by making sure you understand what goes into a quality video. This means evaluating the elements you can see, like design and animation, as well as those you can't, like script, sound, and experience.

Take your time during your selection process. Build a large list of providers, narrow it to a shortlist, and take a week to have conversations with your 3-4 favorites. This extra discovery time will pay off big in the long run.

Do you want your video to stand out from the pack? In the next chapter, you'll learn about compelling techniques that few companies consider.

3. Techniques

The folly of stale and unsuccessful explainers is not usually lack of time, effort, or budget, but rather lack of imagination. In this chapter, you'll learn about the compelling techniques most companies don't know about. Even if your budget is limited and the fanciest of these styles is out of reach, you can use them to inspire visual ideas and think beyond the formulaic. Referencing concrete examples to your producer will help them create a memorable piece. Without falling into the technical weeds, this means understanding the mechanics a little so you can talk the talk.

For insight, take a moment to check out the samples in Resources, or simply google these techniques.

Puppet Animation

This technique, sometimes known as vector animation, is perhaps the most common explainer video style. It's typified by the manipulation of static characters and other still visuals. It's referred to as "puppet" because limbs and other elements are moved about robotically.

The puppet technique is made possible by first designing the characters, using software like Photoshop, and then sliding around the images in Adobe's After Effects, or a similar program. When you see DIY animation in software like PowToon, it's basically a very rough version of this technique. The pro is that puppet is relatively inexpensive, and the con is that it doesn't allow for the dramatic poses and life-like movements you find with high-quality approaches.

Whiteboard Animation

This technique is very popular because it does an excellent job encapsulating an enormous amount of detail. While many explainers are vibrant and exciting, whiteboard exudes coolness, and it makes complex subjects digestible. If you have an intimidating product or service, it might be an ideal fit.

Whiteboard animation was pioneered in the UK by the Royal Society of Animators, or "RSA" for short, and sometimes the technique is referred to as "RSA-style" animation. There are a couple ways to do whiteboard. The first is the classic stop motion method: An artist draws a huge storytelling image on the board, then she is filmed erasing it with an emptied pen. Next, the sequence is run backwards, edited, and sped up, which creates the choppy hand-drawing effect as the elaborate image is revealed. The downside to this process is that it's very time-consuming, and tedious, which it why it's less common for business videos. You have one opportunity to get it right, and screwing it up can mean redrawing everything.

The more common process is a fully animated simulation. Typically, the line and characters are designed in Photoshop and manipulated in After Effects. The drawing hand, which can be turned on or off easily, is made up of a few green-screened poses. The huge advantage of this approach is that it offers leeway for edits, colors, splashes of animation, and other fun effects.

Motion Graphics

One of the most modern-looking techniques, motion graphics offers a ton of creative options. If your brand is sleek and tech-oriented, then this style is worth considering. Also, if you've created infographics, this technique will let you put them into motion and expand their power.

Motion graphics is defined by digital footage and/or animation being used to create the illusion of motion or rotation. Animators use platforms like After Effects and Maxon's Cinema 4D to create in this style.

I've observed that many videos in this style fail to incorporate characters, which are essential to any compelling story. Instead they fall back on text and icons alone. To create a motion graphics video that resonates strongly with human beings, include personas, even if they're iconic representations.

Kinetic Typography

Does your marketing strategy center on trade shows or other noisy events? If so, a kinetic typography, or "dynamic text", video might be a good fit. Kinetic typography refers to the art and technique of expression with animated text (source: JohnnyLee.net).

If you can't use audio, this style can be effective without voice over. That being said, you should avoid sacrificing the audio information stream if you don't absolutely have to. Some of my previous clients and prospects at first sought to create soundless explainers because they were worried that their viewers wouldn't be able to listen at work or in other busy locations. I usually dissuaded them from this route because audio is half, if not more, of video's power.

More importantly, when viewers click on a video, they expect to hear sound. Cutting out audio does not affect whether or not the viewer clicks "play" in the first place. If you're concerned about ease of listening, a better move is including auto-playing/default captions.

Mixed Media

The next few techniques require quite a bit of expertise and labor, and they may be out of reach for startups and entrepreneurs with tight budgets. Still, it's valuable to have them on your radar because they will inspire ideas during your production process, and you can keep them in mind as future possibilities.

The first is mixed media, and it lends itself well to many products and goals. It's particularly strong for offerings that encompass both physical and digital components. The approach lets you use live action to showcase the actual product, and animation to demonstrate the benefits and user experience.

As an example, certain Apple commercials come to mind. The tech giant created iPod and iPhone ads giving their audience a taste for the user experience. Real humans were shown using these products while animated screen capture pop-ups showcased what was happening in the digital void.

Traditional 2D Character Animation

What if you could capture the storytelling power of the classic studios like Warner Bros. and Disney? Although traditional 2D character animation is no small investment, it's much more accessible than it once was.

This technique doesn't have to look childish. All sorts of grown-up companies leverage this approach to add drama and life to their offerings. This technique is IdeaRocket's speciality, and during my time there we used it for tech startups, management consulting firms, and Fortune 500s. To stay on-brand, sometimes we went for the wry and sophisticated angle by designing in the style of *The New Yorker* and other buttoned-up editorial inspirations.

The 2D character animation process is reminiscent of the frame-by-frame approach used by the classic studios. You might have seen pictures or documentaries of old time animators drawing out each and every frame and then running them together to make Bugs Bunny. Though new technology makes the process much less labor-intensive, it lives on in that tradition. Designs are created using software like Photoshop, and then the still images are moved around and manipulated using After Effects or a related program. In between, there's an extra phase where still frames are animated in Adobe's Flash program, which creates fluid character movements and subtle poses.

3D

When you think of 3D animation, the incredible movies of Pixar and Dreamworks might come to mind. These productions require millions of dollars and years of labor. Although stacking up against 3D blockbusters is probably beyond your needs and capabilities, using 3D technology to create truly a memorable explainer is well within reach for many established companies. All the same, few organizations think to go this route. At IdeaRocket, we got the opportunity to create 3D videos for a number of companies, and the style served as a major differentiator.

3D involves first creating and then manipulating rigged characters and objects. Digital cameras, meant to emulate real-life shoots, are positioned to capture different perspectives in the 3D environment. Autodesk's Maya program, a very expansive and complex platform, is the main software used.

Stop Motion

If you really want to be unconventional, stop motion is worth a look. Claymation is the common example, but you can use just about any physical object to create a video using this technique.

The process entails hard work, patience, and expertise. It involves filming a physical object, usually on a flat surface, moving it slightly into a new pose, and filming it again. This is done thousands of times, and then edited together to create the choppy and hypnotic effect.

Out-there movies like *Wallace and Gromit* come to mind, but startups have been known to use this style as well. Business-focused stop motion explainers have included a hand writing in a notebook and moving office items atop a desk. This style sticks with people, and it's worth exploring for the entertainment value if nothing else.

Live Action Formats

Live action covers a lot of ground. Let's go over the formats it handles best.

- **Testimonials**
  Human faces are a great trust builder if you want to tell the story of a customer's journey before, during, and after implementing your product. Though there are successful animations in this vein, live action is a more straightforward route for connecting storyteller and audience.

- **Culture videos**
  Along the same lines, if you're looking to create a culture video to attract new talent or build employee engagement, show the actual people at your company's core.

- **Physical products**
  If you have a physical product, you have to show it.

Takeaways

As the web video space gets noisier, it's more important than ever to stand out. You can avoid sinking time and money into a formulaic and forgettable explainer by exploring unconventional techniques. Going for a memorable style doesn't have to mean reinventing the wheel or breaking the bank. It just means getting inspired and speaking your producer's language a little. While developing your own ideas is invaluable, as you get into production, be open to your producer's input regarding technique. While you know your message better than anyone, your producer will be the one to distill your offering into a visual concept.

When it comes time to write a script, many companies make the mistake of rushing to the blank page. In the next chapter, you'll learn how to build your script's foundation through IdeaRocket's Creative Interview process.

4. Creative Interview

If you plan on writing your explainer script, you're probably wondering what should go into it. Whether you're an accomplished writer or a newbie, the blank page is intimidating. Regardless of how you handle scripting, this chapter will help you pull out the high-level points that will serve as the foundation for your narrative. Compiled by IdeaRocket's creative director Will Gadea, this is the discovery process we used to write nearly every explainer that passed through our studio.

Your explainer will be a snappy high-level overview of your offering. Keeping that in mind, you might notice that the Creative Interview questions are not earth-shattering, and there's only about twenty of them. You might know many of the answers like the back of your hand. That's the point; this discovery exercise is more about removing clutter than adding to it.

As a minor disclaimer, if you read my video marketing book first, these questions will look familiar from the "Message" chapter. I re-interpolated them there because they're valuable in both the context of a marketing campaign and an explainer script. If it's been awhile since you went through these considerations, I think a refresher will be helpful.

Product

As you start pulling out the big ideas that will filter into your script, keep video length top of mind. You will have an introduction and a resolution, and pretty much everything from this discovery process will fall in the middle. That means you have less than 90 seconds to project your message. Working with that time crunch might sound stressful, but don't worry: The constraints will make writing easier.

You can think of your product details as the things you would talk about with a new acquaintance at a big networking event. As such, less is more. Focus on the points that will stick with your audience. When it comes to objections, think of the one or two that you hear all the time.

These are the friction points that you start answering in your head before people finish their protestations.

- **What is the problem your product addresses?**
  Or, how do you alleviate your customer's pain?

- **What are your features and benefits?**
  Focus on 1-2 things, and be specific.

- **What are your differentiators?**
  See above.

- **What are common objections?**
  Or, what are the friction points to understanding?

- **Who is your competition, if anyone?**
  Think of what or who else is competing for both your buyer's money and attention.

- **How do you charge and monetize?**
  If your payment system is convenient, and it's a selling point, you might want to talk about it.

Strategy

These are the most-neglected considerations. By hashing these out, you'll be miles ahead of most companies that create explainers. This is where you'll decide where your video will go and how it will get there. Most importantly, you will nail down your calls to action from the get-go.

- **How will your video be distributed?**
  Think about the viewing environment. A video for online viewers will differ from an event video.

- **What is your objective?**
  Focus on specific, measurable results: leads, sales, users, engagement, comprehension, etc. Going viral is unrealistic and not necessarily desirable. "Viral" is a buzzword for "popular", which is a vague and ungrounded goal.

- **What action(s) should your viewer take?**
  This point is one of the few that will determine success. Instead of fading to black, guide your viewers to an immediate next step. Your call to action will depend on your audience and offering, but generally small steps are most effective. Instead of asking viewers to sign up for a 15-minute consultation, entice them to download an ebook after joining your newsletter.

- **How long will your video be?**
  As covered, 90 seconds is ideal. Longer runtimes tend to experience high drop-off rates and lower views because people decline to make the time investment by clicking "play" in the first place. That being said, if you're dealing with a captive audience in an event, you can usually go longer.

Brand

Here is where you'll make sure your video lives in harmony with your brand. A couple pitfalls I've observed are when high-end products with sleek websites put up low-quality explainers, or when the visual approach completely clashes with a site's aesthetics.

Your brand goes deeper than visuals alone; it projects a personality. Taking a few minutes to hash out brand questions will help ensure that your video gels with everything else.

- **What is your brand personality?**
  Maybe yours is serious, edgy, light-hearted, or academic. Consider how much leeway you have for humor, which can be a great way to engage your audience.

- **What is your brand promise?**
  This is defined by what your users are expecting when they come on your site, and it surrounds all the considerations in this section.

  Regardless of your interaction with an Apple product or store, be it online or brick-and-mortar, you're promised that you'll be greeted with a clean and uncluttered visual experience.

- **Do you have a visual style?**
  Consider the shapes, colors, and user experience of your site, as well as other customer touch points.

- **Do you have a logo?**
  Have a vector version ready before you enter production (usually this file ends with ".eps" or ".ai"). Make sure your video's text doesn't clash with your logo.

Audience

This is the most important section of the Creative Interview. This is where you'll understand your audience's mindset. Not everyone who approaches your site and watches your video will be ready to buy. If you have a big ticket product, other stakeholders may have to enter the equation before they can engage you.

Again, you probably know this stuff. Here's where you'll make sure the important points end up in your script.

- **What are the demographics of your audience?**
  Consider age, gender, education level. . . . These considerations will affect production decisions, like your voice over artist and characters.

- **What seniority are they?**
  This and the next few apply to B2B offerings.

- **Do they need buy-in from superiors before they engage you?**
  Think about the typical decision makers you must nurture.

- **What stage of the sales funnel are they in?**
  Envision where your typical viewer will be on their journey toward becoming a customer. Usually your explainer will live at the top of your funnel, onboarding new visitors to lead status.

- **What is their mindset when approaching your site?**
  Let's dissect this big question into smaller ones: Do they know they have a problem? Do they know what the solution is? Are they just looking for right provider?

Technique

Based on the techniques we covered early, which do you think will best project your message?

Don't worry if you have trouble nailing this down. Your producer will lay out options to guide your decision, and they will probably make a recommendation. Therein lies their expertise. That being said, it's helpful to take a second to consider an ideal visual approach alongside your Creative Interview.

Takeaways

At IdeaRocket, I often felt a mild awkwardness when asking certain Creative Interview questions during kickoff calls. That's because many are elementary and can be ascertained at face value. I realized their importance, however, when company after company struggled to answer these inquiries. Sure, a client or two were unprofessionally oblivious, but most were so caught up in their day-to-day product complexities that they couldn't see the forest for the trees. This is a challenge for all of us. To create a great explainer, or to tell any compelling story for that matter, you must first take a step back. These discovery questions will help you do that.

The Creative Interview is the first cut in a two-part destructive exercise that will help you write your script. The next part is where you or your writer will confront the scary blank page. By using creative fences, you'll develop a powerful narrative.

5. Script

Writers, directors, and actors agree: It's all about the strength of the script. While it's possible to patch up a rough voice over track or choppy animation sequence, no amount of audio-visual trickery will fix a broken script.

To set expectations, I'd be over promising if I said this chapter will make you into a great writer. You have to build your writing muscles through long term exercise. What you'll learn is how to get off and running and put words on the blank page. Quite counterintuitively, it's easiest to move ideas from your mind to your typing hand when you restrain, not expand, your creativity. You'll soon learn why limits are empowering.

This chapter will come in handy even if you plan on hiring out writing, either to a freelancer or to your full-service studio. The takeaways will help you evaluate script drafts and effectively communicate your vision to your writer.

The 4 Narrative Elements

Once again, we'll draw from the writing method used by Will Gadea at IdeaRocket. Here you'll take a step back from the raw business details you'll distill from the Creative Interview. Instead, you'll focus on what makes for a great story.

1. **Characters**

   To tell a story, you pretty much have to use characters. They don't necessarily have to be detailed, or identified by name. You don't have to start your video in the common way, with, "This is Bob...." Instead, you might choose to speak directly to the audience, for example. The perspective you take is where the creativity comes in.

2. **Conflict**

   This is the main challenge your character is experiencing. Ask, "What's wrong with my hero?" The next element, Quest, will be about turning this flaw into a strength. Think of Rudolph's red nose, any

X-Men character, or the ugly duckling. The conflict doesn't necessarily have to be a problem for your character, it can simply be an opportunity to learn something new. Usually this where you filter in the customer pain you determined earlier.

3. Quest

This is your hero's path to the solution. They might reach their destination through a journey of actions or explanation.

4. Resolution

This is where your hero reaches her solution. Perhaps she is left with a new awareness, or an opportunity to continue the conversation.

The Restriction Method

With this method, creativity is the enemy, and you need to put fences on it. Sounds illogical, right?

Here's why it works. When you sit down to write, your brain is filled with a huge, unorganized bramble of ideas. As Will argues, embracing limits removes obstacles. The Restriction Method will help you cut out a multitude of distractions.

Let's use an owl as an example. If I asked you to draw an owl, chances are you'd screw it up. You'd probably give up quickly, or draw some weird bird-like creature. That's understandable: It's a strange animal. Even professional artists have trouble with owls.

Now what if I told you to draw an owl using only circles and triangles. It would still be a challenge, especially if you hate drawing, but all of a sudden it becomes doable. The question goes from "Can you draw an owl?" to "What will your owl look like?"

This is an example of how the simple act of defining limits makes the impossible suddenly approachable. When it comes to video script writing, here is your restriction method:

- **How many characters?**
- **How many locations?**
- **How long is it?**

That's it! Let's dig into each point:

- **Characters**
  Two is much easier to work with than one: You can make one the hero, and the other the villain, loser, or loveable idiot.

- **Locations**
  One logical location makes writing easier. Ideally it's interior so that your background is less distracting, and probably more relevant unless you have an outdoorsy product. More importantly, using one simple location will center attention on your character instead of your background.

- **Length**
  As covered, 90 seconds is probably what you're going for. Runtime is an excellent creative fence.

Once you set these limitations, the next step is developing the 4 narrative elements from earlier.

Audio-Visual Script Template

Using an audio-visual template will help you organize your writing and structure it by scene. Also, it will let you draft visual ideas textually. You can use the first row to set the stage by describing the audio tone and general visual approach.

Check out the below sample from an IdeaRocket's "Animation Is..." explainer, which you can watch in <u>Resources</u>. You can easily recreate this template by building a simple table in Word or Google Docs.

Animation Is... (v.3)
Written by William Gadea

	AUDIO	VISUAL
	The tone is educational but warm, and sometimes wry. The music has a different color and feel for each section.	*The star of the video is the animator, who is also his own subject. The reflexive Escher-esque quality of this is a recurring motif.*
1	Animation is a simulation of movement created by a sequence of images.	We see a bunch of flat images fall one on top of the other, at an increasing pace, to create an animation.
2	When text or graphics are animated we call it . . .	We see shapes and type . . .
3	. . . motion graphics.	. . . that makes the word MOTION GRAPHICS.
4	When a character is introduced we call it . . .	Shapes combine to create a character; the words MOTION GRAPHICS scamper away.

5	. . . character animation.	The character waves to the camera.
6	There are three major techniques in animation.	We see three headings: 2D, 3D, and Stop Motion.
7	2D or 2-dimensional animation is flat artwork that moves.	The 2D heading takes over the screen.
8	During its golden age, traditional animation was drawn on transparent cells, which were photographed over backgrounds, often painted in watercolors.	We see an Oxberry style camera, and an animator shooting a cell. The new cell replaces the old one; we pull out and see the same scene.
9	Today, traditional animators usually work on computers. Instead of drawing on paper or cells, they draw on touch-sensitive monitors.	Again we see a hand drawing a hand.
10	Another kind of 2D computer animation is called puppet animation. Instead of drawing each frame separately like traditional animators do, puppet animators rotate limbs and switch out parts.	We see the Animator get torn apart into bits and then put together again with hinges in joints.
11	The movements in puppet animation are less organic, but puppet animation is cheaper and allows animators to use richer textures.	The Animator starts moving around in a puppet-ish way. His clothes start to become rich and textured.

12	3D or CGI animation is created in computers using 3-dimensional space.	We see X-Y-Z coordinates arrows heading for infinity.
13	CGI artists can model shapes and define how they interact with light.	The drawn character models a 3D version. Different shaders like chrome and glass and cloth get switched out on the Animator.
14	Just as in real anatomy, they put bones into their characters so that they can move them easily.	We see the character get rigged.
15	And just as in a real set, they illuminate their scenes with virtual lights and shoot them with virtual cameras.	We see lights, and textures, and we start moving around the scene.
16	The third and final technique in animation is stop motion.	The word STOP MOTION is created out of photographed objects moving into place.
17	Stop motion animators photograph a subject, then move it slightly. Photograph it, then move it, . . . until the illusion of movement is achieved.	We see a drawn character photograph a scene (that is actually comprised of photographed material), then move to alter it, then go back to the camera, at an increasing pace.
18	These animators work with different media, such as puppets, paint, clay, paper, coffee grinds, . . . nearly anything you can think of.	The animator molds a piece of clay into the likeness of himself. The clay model puckers his lips into a kiss, and raises his eyebrows significantly to his creator. The creator looks

		worried.
19	At IdeaRocket, we use all these techniques to deliver our clients' messages.	A rocket rushes past an inset holding a traditional scene, and then past an inset holding a CGI, but then it skids to a halt before it passes a stop motion inset.
20	Well, except for stop motion. We're still trying to master that one.	We pull into the inset: The clay model has swallowed the Animator. His legs wave as they poke out of the mouth.
21	Contact us to learn more.	The logo animates on and we see the URL: www.IdeaRocketAnimation.com
	Timed at Medium pace: 1:24	

Getting Started

Here are general tips and advice for writing a powerful script. The first few will get you to the starting line.

- **Borrow an opener**
  Watch a video that resonates with you, and "borrow" or re-interpolate their opening line. Maybe you're speaking directly to the audience, talking about your industry, or a problem. On your second pass you can edit your opener and make it fit your offering.

- **Start out rough**
  Don't use perfect wording right away. Use silly adverbs as placeholders if needed. If you're digging for a word to describe how awesome your app is, use "awesome" for now, and circle back to set it right later. This will let you keep up momentum.

- **Time it out**

  At each draft stage, time out your script and include the runtime at the bottom, as per the above example. By the way, your smartphone has a stopwatch. Keeping your runtime top of mind will help you stay on budget by avoiding length overages. If you're outsourcing scripting, mark the runtime of your writer's drafts if they haven't already.

- **Get inspiration**

  If you hit a wall, look to your favorite videos, and go beyond business explainers. Watch short movies, commercials, and virals. Read great stories, even if they come from static content like books, articles, or comics. Getting inspiration from an outside voice will keep your writing flowing, and you'll re-contextualize ideas for your explainer.

- **Read aloud**

  This is an essential writing exercise. The way your writing sounds in your head is almost always a world apart from how it sounds out loud. Keep a natural, medium pace to get an accurate feel for length.

- **Speak to your audience**

  Try to use "you" instead of "programmers" or "accountants", because it builds a stronger connection. This doesn't necessarily mean you shouldn't use a third person perspective to tell your story, but you should break the third wall at some point. If nowhere else, this can happen during your call to action.

- **Intellectualizing is NOT worth complicating**
  This is one of the most common issues I've seen with explainers and marketing in general: Using jargon and $100 words when 25-cent phrases work fine will make you sound dense and pretentious. I'm not saying that you have to focus on the most ignorant layman; if you're audience is specialized, make sure to speak their language. But don't overdo it with too much jargon and overwrought complexity. Demonstrating your experience by telling a compelling story will make you look much smarter than anything else you can do.

- **Don't be afraid of cliches**
  There's a reason cliches are cliches: They work. People know what you mean when you use a lightbulb to represent an idea, or a flying paper airplane to represent communication. Don't go searching for some weird, complex metaphor if you can use an instantly-recognizable device.

- **Use metaphors sparingly**
  Following up on the last point, be careful not to mix up too many metaphors. You don't want to be convoluted. Use no more than one or two.

- **Use superlatives like condiments**
  You wouldn't bury your steak in salt, but you might dash on a little on to enhance the flavor. Treat superlatives the same way. "Sleek, intuitive, easy to use, new, great, seamless, instant" . . . these words are

powerful until they're used in excess, at which point they hurt your message.

- **Create character interaction**
  Instead of a voice over, consider guiding your narrative with a conversation between two or more characters. Few explainers do this, and using this technique would be a major differentiator.

Calls to Action

Your call to action, or CTA, is the one element of your video that you should test, measure, and optimize. Your CTA leads viewers directly to the next step, so it's important to ensure that it's performing. The good news is that it's easy to create several calls to action and slip them in with minimal work or production expense.

Some marketers encourage creating and A/B testing video openers, middle scenes, and closers. I don't recommend it; if you're producing a high-quality video, creating that much additional content is usually prohibitively expensive and extremely labor-intensive. Instead, just focus on your CTA.

You'll lead your audience to the next stage at your video's end frame. You should leave viewers with a destination URL and voice over instructions. Since the content is static, it's easy to create a few different versions.

When you're nearly finished with your script, write down 3-5 action ideas. Some good ones might include, "Click here to download our whitepaper [or ebook]", or "Join our newsletter."

Early on, let your video producer know that you would like to create a few different versions with alternate CTAs.

Additional still frames and voice over ending lines should incur minimal overages, if any.

As most marketers will affirm, it's best to assume nothing. Test your CTAs in the same context before drawing conclusions. As we covered, aim for simple actions. Getting a new viewer to download your whitepaper and enter your email list is a lot easier than getting them to agree to a 15-minute consultation with a salesperson.

Linking

If you're on YouTube, you can only link to an external source in the description, and your overlay buttons must direct to other YouTube pages. Hosts like Wistia make it easy to include CTA buttons within in the video. If you don't want to deal with overlays, when you showcase the video on your site, feature a big button next to the player that directs users to a particular action.

DIY Storyboard

Here is a quick and easy process for creating a do-it-yourself storyboard template using PowerPoint. It will help you rough out your ideas.

Even if you're hiring out design, a rough storyboard will be a helpful visualization tool. Just make sure your producer can edit and give you their unclouded concept. After all, that's why you're hiring them!

1. In PowerPoint, create a completely blank slide and duplicate it 8-12 times.

2. Insert text boxes at the bottom of each slide, and copy/paste each scene from your audio script to each slide.

3. Click File > Print. Under "Print What", select "6 slides per page". Click "Print".

4. Use stick figures and sketch out your ideas for each scene. Have fun!

Takeaways

As a marketing exercise, writing your explainer script is bigger than the sum of its parts. This process will help you better understand your product and the best way to position it. Even if you ultimately hire out writing, I recommend taking a stab at a first draft. If nothing else, it will get your creative juices flowing and it will inspire ideas.

To make this task approachable, funnel your raging river of creativity into a manageable stream. Do this through the Restriction Method. This approach is common in many other creative mediums; top designers, for example, often say that their work is 80% destructive.

From there, take simple actions to get words down on paper. Editing is a surpassable hill compared to the mountain that is the blank page.

Now you might be wondering what production actually entails. How do you make sure that your provider creates a video that will fulfill your goals? How do you ensure your process goes smoothly? You'll find out in the next chapter.

6. Production

Congrats, you're done with the hard part! It's time to make your video. In this chapter, you'll learn how to ensure a smooth and worry-free production process. This means preparing your team, setting expectations, and giving your producer the right direction and resources so they can create a stellar end product. In addition, you'll learn how to get a high-quality and affordable voice over, and you'll understand the easy enhancements that will add a ton of drama and energy to your piece.

Preparation

At IdeaRocket, most of the projects I managed went smoothly because we set expectations early and helped our clients prepare for the production process. The snafus and horror stories I've heard are usually tied to both parties, producer and client, being vague about their expectations and goals.

To ensure a smooth process and a successful video, here are a few straightforward tips:

- **Be clear on strategy**
  Be upfront about not just what you want to do, but why you want to do it. Circle back to the questions you answered earlier about your business objectives and audience.

- **Be clear on branding**
  Your producer can guess about your brand personality, but they won't know for sure until you lay it out for them. Do this early so they don't go too far in the wrong direction.

- **Involve stakeholders early**
  This one is huge. If you're a founder or some other position in a startup, chances are the approval process will be pretty straightforward. However, if you're in a large organization, waiting for so-and-so to sign off on a script or storyboard will throw a wrench in the gears. Late-stage backtracking can be costly and time-consuming. To avoid hiccups, get all critical stakeholders involved from the start.

- **Assign a point person**

  The production process does not lend itself to trickle-in feedback that comes from different people at different times. For this reason, it's most efficient to give consolidated edits at each key draft stage. To make this easy, assign a point person to compile notes from your team. If needed, set up weekly review meetings.

- **Have comfortable deadlines**

  Video production is a time-intensive process. The "I need it yesterday" ethos won't do you any favors unless there's a legitimate reason for it, like an event. A comfortable working period, within reason, often results in a higher-quality video at no additional cost. If you give them enough breathing room, your creatives will get excited about their ideas, and they'll tack on major enhancements. For example, at IdeaRocket, there were a few occasions when we had some wiggle room, and we decided to give our clients an original musical score at no additional charge.

- **Go hard, go soft**

  Try to balance your "must haves" with your "nice to haves". Many creative directors do the same thing with their subordinates: They pass along hard notes, which are required changes, and soft notes, which are optional. You should do the same because it will ensure your producer meets your most important objectives while empowering them with creative ownership.

- **Don't censor yourself**
  Your producer should know how to create the vessel for your message, including the storytelling, color, line, and timing. There's nothing wrong with deferring to them in regard to these elements. But at the end of the day, you know your message better than anyone, so don't be afraid to give criticism and honest feedback on anything and everything.

Voice over Considerations

Voice over, or VO, will have a huge effect on the impact of your video. You might choose to cast it yourself, or maybe your producer will present auditioned artists for your selection. As we covered earlier, if you have a tight budget, you might be able to bring costs down by approaching an a la carte studio, or freelancer, with your script and pre-recorded VO.

Below are high level considerations you should keep in mind before entering the voice over marketplace. In the following two sections, you'll learn how to effectively cast, audition, and hire.

- **Make sure your script is approved**
  It's a pain dealing with voice over retakes. After a couple of them, your artist will usually want additional fees. Make sure your script is set in stone before moving ahead.

- **Consider audience demographics**
  If your video is about a Pinterest app, then you probably don't want a gruff-sounding male voice. If you have a balanced male/female audience ratio, a great strategy is using different genders for the hero

and the voice over: You might go with a female hero and a male voice over artist, or vice versa.

- **Consider tone**
  Is your narrative witty, funny, serious, academic, . . .? Your tone should inform who you hire. If your subject matter is complicated, you might want a calm, communicative tone. If it's an unsexy subject, like accounting, then you might want to add excitement with a high-energy, youthful voice.

- **Consider brand**
  Your chosen voice should gel with your other marketing initiatives. If your voice is a radical brand departure, make sure your site, blog, and overall public presence will follow suit.

Casting

The marketplace for voice over talent is notoriously competitive, which is good news for you. When it comes time to hire freelancers, you might think of Upwork and Fiverr first. Instead, I recommend Voice123, a network that's tailored specifically to VO.

Voice123 lets you search by artist age, gender, accent, and tone, and it's easy to rate artists and share auditions. It features professional talent, including many Hollywood and commercial people, but you won't have to break the bank.

Here is how your VO casting process should go:

1. Post a casting call and include a custom demo with the first 2-3 lines of your script

2. Invite 15-20 actors

3. Review and shortlist 2-3 auditions

4. Get feedback from your team

5. Make a decision and offer the job

Here is a typical casting call I used many times at IdeaRocket:

We seek a female actress to voice an explainer video for a social money-sharing app. The video is designed to drive sign-ups during the product's initial roll out.

Your tone should be calm, approachable, yet energetic.

The video will be 90 seconds or less. Our rate is $300, and for this we would like 3 initial takes, and up to three retakes for rewrites or performance, which we hopefully won't need. Further retakes will be compensated at $75 per.

We look forward to your audition!

How much should you pay?
According to Voice123, the average price for a 2-minute web video is $100. If you're on a tight budget, feel free to go lower and see what auditions come in.

Evaluating Auditions and Recording
When it comes time to review your voice over auditions, here's what you should listen for:

- **Cadence**
  How is your artist's pace? Does it sound smooth and natural, is it choppy, or does it drag on? Keep your

video length in mind: Is this person's pace going to do the job in 90 seconds?

- **Tone**
  Does the audition match the tone you specified in your casting call?

- **Enunciation**
  Can you understand what they're saying? Do they exude clarity or eat their words?

- **Sound quality**
  This is big. Listen carefully for technical qualities; if it's crappy in the audition, it will be the same on the recording. Make sure the levels are consistent, and that the audition is free of echo, pops, and other artifacts.

Because it's such a competitive marketplace, I've rarely if ever had a negative experience with an artist. I think you'll find that most are responsive and professional. That being said, for maximum efficiency you should hire fast, and if needed, fire fast. It's easy enough to bring on new talent if someone isn't working out, but sticking with a flaky VO artist will screw up your process.

Video Tech Specs

Most web videos are produced at a 16:9 aspect ratio, and at a physical size of 1280 by 720 pixels. Your producer will probably be designing to those specs, and if your video's main home is on the web, then there's not much cause for concern.

If, however, your video will be shown on a big screen at a tradeshow or another event, or you're making a television commercial, then you may need larger dimensions at 1920 x 1080 pixels. If you're in this boat, make sure to let your producer know at the outset to avoid being forced to recreate your video. Since the work files are larger, occasionally studios charge a nominal fee for the expanded size.

Draft Stages

Here you'll get a basic rundown of the typical animation draft stages. This will help you know what to expect. The phases will depend on your producer and technique.

To avoid backtracking, make sure your script and voice over are approved before moving onto design, animation, and sound.

1. **Style Frames**

   If your producer is developing an original visual concept, often they'll showcase it with a style frame before developing it fully. This is a still image with some characters and a background. If you're using a well-known style, like whiteboard animation, you probably won't experience this phase.

2. **Storyboard**

   Many producers submit storyboards as the first visual draft. Each scene is portrayed in still images, and it's mapped to each scene in the audio script. A professional storyboard should be like a blueprint for the video; it indicates transitions and movement, and it shows enough detail to quickly visualize how the video will play out.

3. **Animatic**

   A more-developed draft stage, which IdeaRocket uses, is an animatic. It's a storyboard with voice over, rough design, and basic movements. It's just a little more work than a storyboard and it's much more revealing.

4. **Layout Animatic**

   Depending on the style, sometimes there's a stage called the *layout animatic*. It's inherent to a high-quality frame-by-frame technique. At this stage, the movement is about 90% in place.

5. **Animation**

   This where you'll see complete design and full movement. Everything is in place for the sound effects, and sometimes music.

6. **Final**

   Music and sound effects are added. Since these audio elements are tied to the timing of the animated movements, they usually come last.

Revisions

I've had clients ask for late-stage edits that are tough to pull off without redoing the whole video. A classic example is changing the gender of the main character once we're at the animation phase.

Ease of change depends on the nature of the retake and the technique. A late-stage character redo in puppet animation might be easier than doing the same thing in a high-quality 2D piece. Without trying to anticipate every possible revision under the sun, I'd like to give you a handy framework for envisioning the animation process. . . .

It's like building a house. You might consider the foundation as the script and voice over, design as the first floor, animation the second, and music and sound effects as the roof. Making changes to the foundation becomes quite labor-intensive once everything else sits on top of it.

Also, what seems easy is not always. An example is making a character walk; this seems like it would be straightforward, right? I thought so too, before I knew better.

Sure, you can make a cheap imitation of walking, but there is a tremendous amount of physical nuance in the way the human body moves. Emulating this movement in a remotely accurate way requires a ton of time and expertise. The best way to avoid creating an overly-ambitious vision is to get your producer's opinion early on.

Music

If you think back to your favorite movies, or even mediocre ones, there aren't many instances where music hurts the experience. It's usually a positive enhancement. That said, a melody may or may not be right for your video, and you should compare your piece with and without it. After creating many whiteboard videos, for example, we found that most of the time, music undercuts the calmness of the style. There's a real simplicity to whiteboard, and a tune can make it feel hectic.

Often your producer will give you a few tracks to consider based on their recommendations, or you may choose to do your own exploring. There are plenty of excellent royalty-free music libraries out there. A few of the top sites are NeoSounds, Shockwave-Sound, and AudioJungle. To compare tracks, you can listen online and then download demo versions, which are lower-quality and usually contain an audio watermark. Listen to your shortlisted tracks as your video plays and get feedback from your team.

Original Score

An original score can add a powerful dramatic dimension to your explainer. A score is written to hit certain cues, and when done right, it will enhance the conflict, climax, and resolution of your piece. If you're interested in going this route, be sure to inform your producer early. The composer should get to work as soon as you have the timing locked in, which usually happens at the animation stage.

Be clear with your composer about your brand, strategy, and production process. Point out the points in your script that the music should emphasize. It helps to send them sample tracks.

Upwork is a great resource for composers. Rates can vary, but I'd say $500-$1,000 is pretty reasonable for a 90-second video. Some studios might offer an original score as an option, but most don't. If you'd like to include one, be proactive about it.

Sound Effects

Sound effects will add an unmatched layer of energy to any video, yet they're often underused if not completely neglected. They include swooshes, bangs, pings, and anything you can imagine (Adam West's 1960s *Batman* show comes to mind).

Like an original score, your sound effects will emphasize important moments, like when your product enters the story, or the hero finds her solution. Best of all, adding them is relatively cheap and easy; most video editing programs come with thousands. When your video is nearly completed, be persistent with your producer to ensure they include this enhancement.

Takeaways

Like good headstrong creatives, at IdeaRocket we privately hemmed and hawed when clients came back at us with revisions. In hindsight, we were right to complain only about 60% of the time, and that's a biased figure. After implementing the requested "40%", we'd find that the changes were spot-on by the time we got to full animation.

Your production process is a bit of a balancing act. You know your message, but your producer is the one who has to make it come to life. With that in mind, make sure to equitably weigh your "must haves" with your "nice to haves". The creative process isn't always linear, but a little preparation and background knowledge will help you avoid major headaches. Furthermore, speaking the language of your creatives will enable you to communicate your vision. Be proactive and make sure your producer includes the small, often-neglected enhancements that will increase your video's impact.

7. Video Marketing

You're well on your way to an awesome video. Now how do you distribute it? What host should you choose? What ROI should you expect?

We'll answer all these questions and many more in the companion book:

Don't Go Viral
The Video Marketing Growth Path for Startups and Entrepreneurs

You'll learn how to launch an effective video marketing campaign. Here are some things we'll cover:

- **Distribution Strategies, Tools, and Hacks**
  Get an ever-growing library of specific methods for increasing your conversions, sales, and audience.

- **Finding Target ROI**
  Use a simple 5-step process; compare performance to related companies; model success.

- **Fitting Video to Your Customer Funnel**
  Don't squander this medium's power; show your video to the right audience at the right time.

For more details, head to Amazon via this shortlink: www.SaleSchema.com/DanAuthorPage

Key Takeaways

As marketers, entrepreneurs, and businesspeople, we're profoundly lucky to be living in our current era. Not long ago, video was a tool for only well-established companies with sizeable budgets. Now the most powerful marketing medium is at your fingertips.

We can set aside all the data-driven explanations for video's effectiveness; we're familiar with its power from a lifetime of beloved movies and shows. While mimicking the dazzle of Hollywood and television is probably beyond your needs, you can capture a bit of this same magic in your explainer.

At the core, this means telling a compelling story, which requires characters. It means breaking the cycle of formulaic videos by using a memorable technique. Thankfully, you can do this without overspending or going overly conceptual. To create a successful video, start with your message as a foundation, and funnel your high-level points into your script. Fence in your creative urges with the Restriction Method for writing, and sculpt your ideas into a coherent narrative. Once you've surpassed the barrier of the blank page, writing becomes approachable.

You can choose how hands-on you want to be, based on your skills, budget, and availability. Whatever you choose to do yourself or offload, knowing what to expect for your production process will save you from headaches. Speaking your producer's language will get you to a powerful end product.

Congrats on reaching the explainer milestone. You've probably worked hard to get here. Now go tell the world your story!

Would You Do Me a Solid?

If you found this book helpful, it would be awesome if you would post a short review on Amazon. You'll be helping future readers know what to expect.

Head to the below link, then click on the *Explainer* book:
www.SaleSchema.com/DanAuthorPage

Thanks in advance!

Special Thanks

This book was made possible through the insight and experience of Will Gadea and the IdeaRocket team. They're the best in the game.

Check out their portfolio at :
www.IdeaRocketAnimation.com.

About the Author

Dan Englander is a New York-based author and entrepreneur. As the first employee and Senior Account Manager, Dan helped launch IdeaRocket, the premier studio for high-quality animated explainer videos. He brought in business and managed productions for Fortune 500s and startups like Venmo.

He's the founder of Sales Schema, a site that helps companies win by melding sales and digital marketing. He's the author of *Mastering Account Management* and other business books. In addition, he teaches high-level online courses on B2B sales and marketing.

Previously, Dan was Account Coordinator at DXagency, where he increased digital exposure for clients like Monster Cable and Marc Ecko. He's a decent living room guitarist and he makes a mean paella.

www.ingramcontent.com/pod-product-compliance
Lightning Source LLC
Chambersburg PA
CBHW070932180526
45168CB00003B/1042